Weather

Rain

by Brienna Rossiter

I0886225

FOCUS READERS

SCOUT

www.focusreaders.com

Copyright © 2020 by Focus Readers, Lake Elmo, MN 55042. All rights reserved. No part of this book may be reproduced or utilized in any form or by any means without written permission from the publisher.

Focus Readers is distributed by North Star Editions:
sales@northstareditions.com | 888-417-0195

Produced for Focus Readers by Red Line Editorial.

Photographs ©: Olesia Bilkei/Shutterstock Images, cover, 1; andreiuc88/Shutterstock Images, 4, 16 (top left); Vadym Zaitsev/Shutterstock Images, 7 (top); Romrodphoto/Shutterstock Images, 7 (bottom); Anastasia-G/Shutterstock Images, 9; FamVeld/Shutterstock Images, 11; fon.tepsoda/Shutterstock Images, 13; ND700/Shutterstock Images, 15 (top); Lisa S./Shutterstock Images, 15 (bottom), 16 (top right); Kotin/Shutterstock Images, 16 (bottom left); Detailfoto/Shutterstock Images, 16 (bottom right)

Library of Congress Cataloging-in-Publication Data
Names: Rossiter, Brienna, author.
Title: Rain / by Brienna Rossiter.
Description: Lake Elmo, MN : Focus Readers, [2020] | Series: Weather | Audience: K to grade 3. | Includes index.
Identifiers: LCCN 2018051345 (print) | LCCN 2018052060 (ebook) | ISBN 9781644930076 (pdf) | ISBN 9781641859288 (ebook) | ISBN 9781641857901 (hardcover) | ISBN 9781641858595 (pbk.)
Subjects: LCSH: Rain and rainfall--Juvenile literature.
Classification: LCC QC924.7 (ebook) | LCC QC924.7 .R67 2020 (print) | DDC 551.57/7--dc23
LC record available at https://lccn.loc.gov/2018051345

Printed in the United States of America
Mankato, MN
May, 2019

About the Author

Brienna Rossiter is a writer and editor who lives in Minnesota. She loves learning random facts by reading books, going to museums, and traveling to new places.

Table of Contents

cloud
drop

What Is Rain?

Rain is water.

Rain falls from **clouds**.

Rain falls as **drops**.

Many drops fall.

They hit the ground.

They make **puddles**.

puddle

How Rain Forms

Clouds are made of
water drops.
The drops hang in the air.

Some drops grow.

They get heavier.

They fall from the sky.

Kinds of Rain

A drizzle is light rain.

It has small drops.

A downpour is heavy rain.

The rain falls fast.

The rain has big drops.

Too much rain can make

a **flood**.

downpour

flood

Glossary

clouds

flood

drops

puddles

Index